LEARNING

D1716780

MY BOOK OF
Gymnastics
HEALTH & MOVEMENT

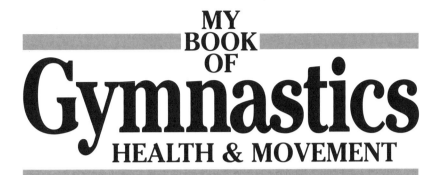

by Amanda Durrant

dedicated to Laura and Helen

photographs by Chris Fairclough

Thomson Learning • New York

My Book of Gymnastics: Health and Movement

Picture Acknowledgments
The publishers wish to thank the following for providing illustrations for use in this book:
Simon Brutv (Allsport) 18; David Cannon (Allsport) 23; Yann Guichaoua (Allsport) 29;
David Leah (Allsport) 27; Bob Martin (Allsport) 14; Richard Martin (Allsport) 25; Gray Mortimore (Allsport) 17;
Tony Stone Worldwide 13. All the other photographs are by Chris Fairclough.

The artwork on pages 4, 5, and 21 is by Mike Gordon; and on pages 18-19 by John Yates.

First published in the
United States in 1993 by
Thomson Learning
115 Fifth Avenue
New York, NY 10003

First published in 1993 by
Wayland (Publishers) Limited

Library of Congress Cataloging-in-Publication Data applied for

ISBN: 1-56847-125-4

Printed in Italy

Contents

Getting Started

Gymnastics is a great sport! It is fun and it is good for your health – as long as you follow some simple rules. Gymnastics helps to keep your body fit, flexible, and strong. Many of the exercises you practice will help you excel in other activities and sports, too.

Posture

Helen has good posture. She stands up straight, relaxes her shoulders, and pulls in her stomach and bottom. ▶

Bad posture harms your joints and makes it harder to breathe and digest food properly. From this boy and his dog, you can see that it looks terrible, too! ▶

Safety

To keep yourself and other gymnasts safe, you must follow simple safety rules.

- Take off your jewelry before you start.

- If you have long hair, tie it back.

- Always warm up and cool down properly.

These gymnasts are wearing suitable clothes that will not restrict their movement. ▼

▲ Never try an exercise that is too difficult for you – you might hurt yourself!

▲ Wear the correct clothes for your activity. You should *not* dress like this!

Warming Up

Gymnasts do many stretching exercises to warm up their muscles. Muscles do not work well when they are cold and tight. When they are warm and stretched, the body is more supple. If you warm up properly, you are less likely to injure yourself. These exercises should take you 15 minutes.

◀ Sanjay is warming up by relaxing his shoulders and tilting his head from side to side.

Now he is stretching his arm and shoulder muscles by making large forward and backward circles. ▶

Laura sits with her legs together. She slides her hands slowly toward her feet and back again. ▼

▲ Paul keeps his back straight, puts his hands on his hips, and leans to the left and the right.

▲ Da Hae slides both hands down one leg toward her ankle. She'll do that on her other leg, too.

Naomi wiggles her fingers and shakes her feet. ▼

▲ Rebecca starts with little jumps, and then jumps higher and higher. She jumps as high as she can.

1 Matthew lies on his stomach, resting on his elbows. **2** Then he pushes backward and **3** curls into a ball.

Now you are ready to start your gymnastics.

Walking

Walking is good exercise. It helps your blood flow and strengthens your muscles. Most people walk at least a little bit every day. Try walking with tiny steps – and then GIANT steps. Try walking backward, swinging your arms for balance.

Can you walk while balancing a beanbag on your head, as Leila is doing here? Now see if you can walk backward with the beanbag on your head. ▶

Running

Running makes your heart pump faster and your lungs work harder. If you run often, your heart and lungs will become stronger. You will not get winded easily because your stamina will have improved. Gymnasts need stamina, as well as strength.

Matthew is running as fast as he can. He is running on his toes, lifting his knees high and punching the air with his arms. ▶

1 Helen is running slowly with small steps **2** and then more quickly with big steps. See how your arms and legs move faster as your speed increases. **3** Try running backward, but be careful!

Bending

Have you ever watched gymnasts on television? They are so flexible that they look as if they are made of rubber! You can improve your suppleness by practicing these exercises.

Sanjay is practicing a sitting bend. Sit with your knees and feet together and your hands comfortably behind you. ▼

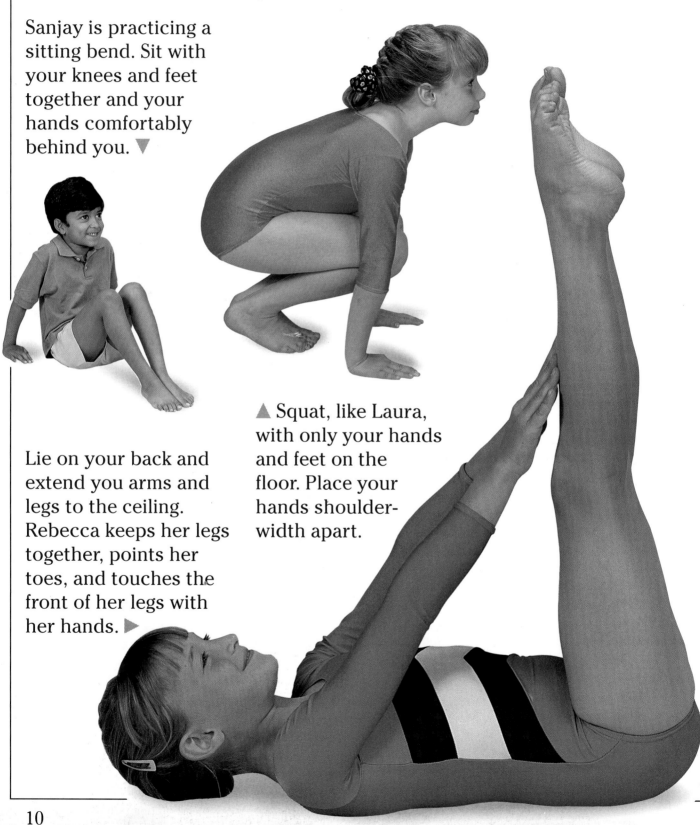

▲ Squat, like Laura, with only your hands and feet on the floor. Place your hands shoulder-width apart.

Lie on your back and extend you arms and legs to the ceiling. Rebecca keeps her legs together, points her toes, and touches the front of her legs with her hands. ▶

▲ Matthew is kneeling, keeping his torso erect, his legs together, and his arms out straight.

▲ Here he is lying on his stomach with his hands under his chin. Bend your knees and point your toes toward the ceiling, keeping your legs together.

▲ Geoff stretches his arms, spreads his legs apart, and turns his feet and knees out. How long can you comfortably stay like this?

▲ Helen is making a bridge to show the suppleness of her back. Your teacher will support you until you can do this on your own.

Stretching

Here are some more stretching exercises for you to practice. Gymnasts stretch on all pieces of apparatus and on the floor. This improves balance, and gives a gymnast style.

Rebecca is holding a difficult stretch. Try doing this yourself – while keeping a relaxed smile on your face! ▶

Geoff is making a star shape. You can do this lying on your back, too. ▼

◀ Da Hae is stretching up with her feet together, arms straight, and fingers closed. You can try this exercise lying on your stomach and then on your back.

Sliding

Sliding exercises take practice. Try doing these movements until they become steady and controlled.

Kneel and place your hands on the floor. Slowly slide your hands forward until you are lying flat. ▼

▲ From a leaning position, slide one foot along until both feet are together. At the same time, bring your arms down.

We can slide on other surfaces, such as ice (ice-skating), water (waterskiing), and snow (skiing). This skier is sliding very fast! ▼

Pushing and Pulling

These exercises test your strength. Geoff and Laura are pushing and pulling to make their bodies travel backward and forward across the floor.

▲ Lie on the floor on your back. Bend your knees and push away with your feet and hands. You will move backward.

Lie on your stomach. Pull both your hands against the floor at the same time. Your body will move forward. ▼

◀ This Olympic gymnast has to push and pull his body weight on the rings. He has to be very strong to do this.

Creeping and Crawling

◀ Can you creep about on tiptoe, slowly and quietly?

Take short steps at first. Then take long steps, moving your arms forward and backward, bending and stretching as you move. Paul looks as if he is about to pounce on something! Try creeping backward just as slowly.

Leila is crawling on all fours, like a cat. Like Paul, she takes small steps and then stretches into bigger steps. Now crawl backward, but be careful not to bump into anything! ▶

Turning

If you start to add up the number of times you turn during the day, you will soon lose count. We often turn to change the direction of our body using our hands, feet, knees, seat, and hands and knees.

▲ Sanjay practices different turns. Keep your eyes open when you do turns so you do
not fall!

Spinning

◄▲ Naomi and Helen are practicing spins. If you increase the speed of a turn, it becomes a spin. During a spin, the body is much tighter than it is in a turn.

16

◀ Geoff practices spinning on one foot. If he folds his arms across his body, he will spin even faster.

This gymnast at the Barcelona Olympics is spinning through the air. She will open her arms to slow the spin before she lands. ▶

Rolling

Naomi is rolling sideways. Her legs are together; her stomach and bottom are pulled in. She stretches her arms over her head. ▶

From the squatting position, **1** Helen lifts her bottom, tucks her chin in, pushes off with her feet and then her hands, and **2** rolls forward onto the back of her shoulders. **3** She finishes sitting in a tucked position.

Try different endings to your sommersaults, such as squatting or standing.

1 . . . . **2** . . . . . . **3** . . .

Jumping

This Olympic long jumper jumps high and far. He can jump more than 26 feet. ▶

How tall are you? How many of you and your friends laid end to end could he jump over?

Here are some jumping footprints. See if you can follow them.

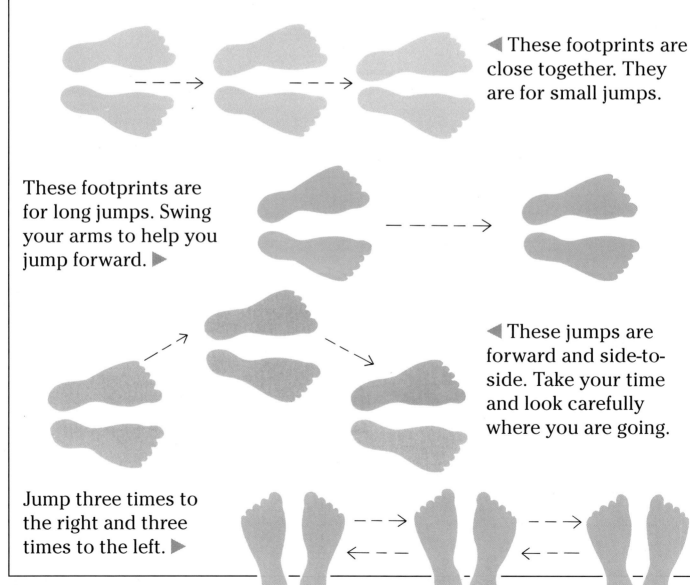

◀ These footprints are close together. They are for small jumps.

These footprints are for long jumps. Swing your arms to help you jump forward. ▶

◀ These jumps are forward and side-to-side. Take your time and look carefully where you are going.

Jump three times to the right and three times to the left. ▶

Hopping

Hopping is jumping on one leg. You can hop forward, backward, sideways, and in place.

Rebecca is hopping in place. Remember to keep your arms wide and one knee in front of you. Your body should be balanced and tight. ▶

Which of these hopping patterns do you find the most difficult? Try them first on your right leg and then on your left.

1 Hopping forward ▼

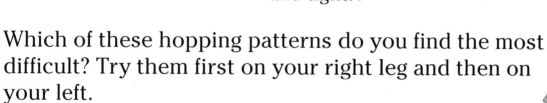

4 Hopping forward and backward ▼

2 Hopping in a curve ▼

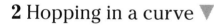

3 Hopping backward ▼

Hopping can make you tired because your muscles have to work very hard. Do not overdo it!

Skipping

Skipping is a combination of walking and hopping. At the end of each step, take a short hop on the same foot.

Can you lift your knees one at a time as you skip forward with your arms outstretched? ▶

Now try skipping backward.

Follow Geoff, and learn how to skip with a rope.

1 Start with the rope resting on the floor behind you, close to your heels.

2 Swing the rope behind you and up over your head.

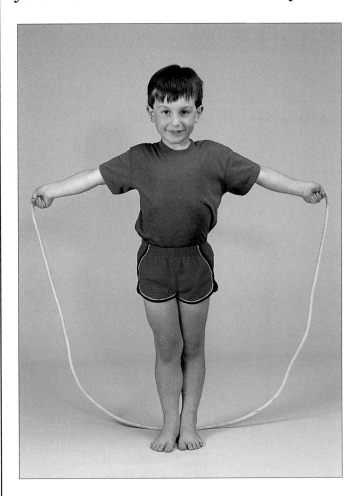

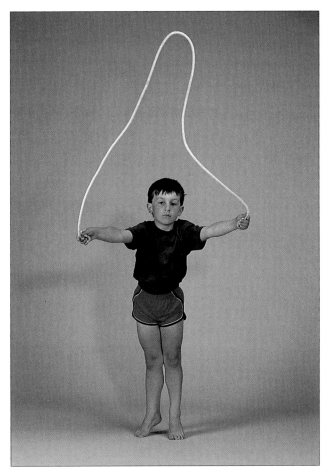

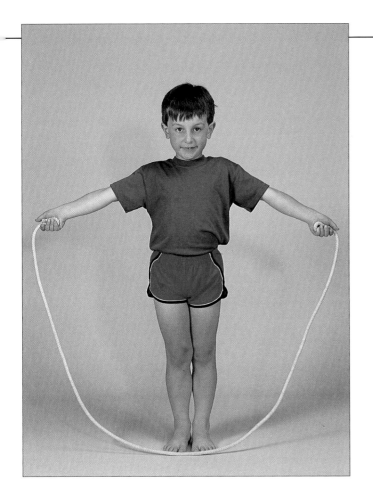

3 Let the rope rest just in front of your feet. **4** Jump over the rope.

Now start all over again. Once you have mastered skipping forward without letting the rope stop, practice skipping backward.

Make sure you choose a rope that is the right length for you. A rope that is too long or too short can make skipping difficult! ▶

Balancing

Balance is being able to hold your body still without falling over. We need balance just to stand. Try standing on one leg. Now close your eyes and try to balance. It is hard not to wobble! Gymnasts need to balance on various parts of their bodies and be able to make many different shapes. How many different shapes can you make? Try counting from one to ten when you are balancing during each position you make with your body.

Naomi practices a similar exercise to Geoff's, but she is straightening her raised leg and lifting it to the side. ▶

◀ Geoff balances on one leg. To do this, he squeezes the muscles in his left leg and raises his right knee. At the same time, he points his right foot and stretches his arms wide.

◀ Da Hae is balancing on one foot and both hands. She points her left foot toward the ceiling. How high can you lift your leg?

Helen's exercise is similar to Da Hae's, but she keeps one knee on the ground. She lifts her hip and points her toes to keep her leg straight. ▷

Helen balances with both hands and feet off the mat. She stretches her arms, points her toes, and holds her stomach in tight. ▷

▲ Rebecca slides one leg behind her and points her toes. Her front leg is bent and she is sitting on her heel. When you try this, stretch your arms wide and keep your back straight.

▲ You use your balance in many activities, like riding a bike. When you first learn, you will probably wobble! This Olympic gold medalist can cycle at high speeds with good control.

Movement and Expression

Gymnastics is a wonderful sport for allowing you to show lots of different feelings. Different movements allow you to express different emotions. Happy movements can be jumping, hopping, leaping, and turning. Try a happy dance routine using some of these movements.

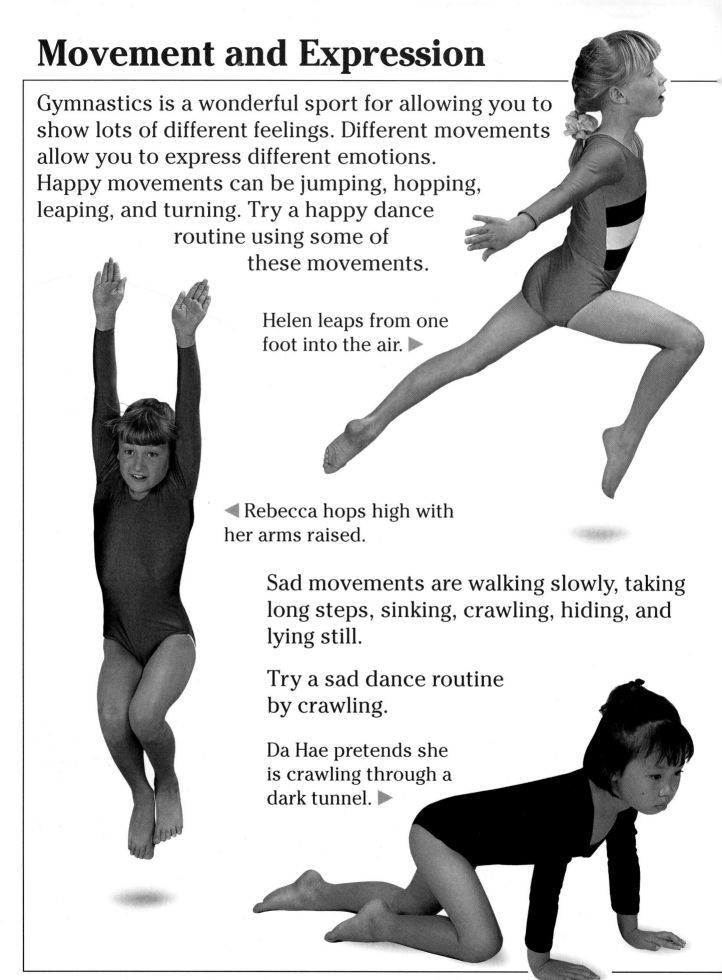

Helen leaps from one foot into the air. ▶

◀ Rebecca hops high with her arms raised.

Sad movements are walking slowly, taking long steps, sinking, crawling, hiding, and lying still.

Try a sad dance routine by crawling.

Da Hae pretends she is crawling through a dark tunnel. ▶

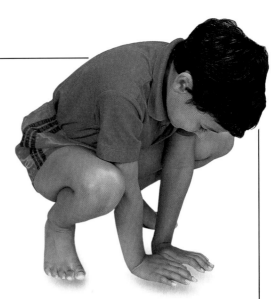

▲ Laura curls up into a tiny ball.

Matthew sinks slowly to the ground. ▶

You may have watched gymnasts on television doing floor routines to music. Sometimes they twirl colorful ribbons or throw clubs high into the air. They show lots of different expressions.

This gymnast is performing rhythmic gymnastics. These exercises allow gymnasts to express many different moods.

Ball Skills

These children are practicing lots of different ball skills. If you practice them hard and keep your eye on the ball, you will find it much easier to play ball games such as football, baseball, tetherball, volleyball, and tennis. Can you think of any others?

5 Throwing the ball with two hands and then one hand.

4 Catching the ball and holding it close to you.

1 Rolling the ball forward and backward.

2 Rolling the ball along your legs with your fingers.

3 Bouncing the ball with two hands.

6 Kicking the ball with the inside of your foot.

7 Running with the ball.

8 Stopping the ball with your foot.

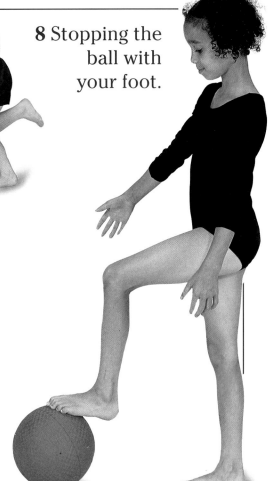

These men are playing volleyball. You need to be a skillful ball player to be good at this game, so you need lots of practice.

When you are playing ball games, remember to be a good sport. Do not keep the ball to yourself too much – pass it around and share it with other people. Congratulate people if they do well – and do not be angry if they make a mistake. If there is something you cannot do, keep practicing until you improve. In all sports, do the best you can and, above all, enjoy them!

Apparatus – Box Top

When gymnasts vault over a box or a horse, they have to get on (mount) and get off (dismount) with great control. Here are some simple mounts and dismounts for you to learn.

Mounting ▲
Jump onto the box top, landing first on your hands and then on your knees. Try again, jumping harder and landing farther along the box top.

Dismounting ▼
Jump off carefully. Bend your knees outward as you land. Stretch up tall and straight to finish.

Rolling Off ▲
Lean over the box top and place your hands on the mat. Lean farther, tuck in your chin, roll over, and land in a squat position.

Apparatus – Climbing Frame

Climbing helps to make you strong. Look carefully where you are going. Stretch up, pull with your hands and push with your feet. Hold on tightly. Climb back down slowly and carefully.

Apparatus – Beam

The balance beam helps you to improve your balance and coordination. Learn to do exercises on the floor or a bench before trying a full-size beam.

▲ How the experts do it!

Balancing ▲
Paul is stretching his body to balance. It helps him to keep still. Try straightening your leg. Keep looking to the front.

Turning ▼
Naomi stretches her arms wide and makes a full turn. Try turning on the balls of your feet, with your heels off the bench. Can you turn with your arms up straight, close to your ears? Keep stretching!

Pulling and Sliding (Traveling) ▼
Sanjay lies on his stomach, holding the sides of the bench in front of him. He pulls with his arms and his body slides forward.

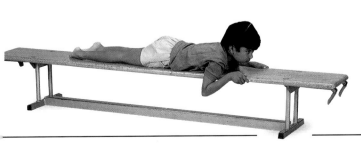

Glossary

Apparatus Equipment used for exercise.

Balance To be able to hold your body still, without falling over.

Balance Beam A narrow platform on which experienced gymnasts perform routines.

Bench A wooden platform, which is wider than a beam and closer to the ground, on which young gymnasts perfect their skills.

Control To be in charge of your body so that you can perform an exercise without wobbling.

Digest To break down food within your body to make use of all the nutrients.

Dismount To get off an object.

Emotions Your feelings, such as sadness or happiness.

Flexible Being able to make your body bend easily.

Horse A piece of equipment that gymnasts vault over.

Joints The parts of your body where two or more bones join together, such as your knees.

Mount To get on an object.

Posture The way you hold your body.

Routine A group of exercises performed one after another.

Rhythmic Gymnastics Gymnastics performed to music and using a hoop, ball, ribbon, or clubs without acrobatics. Artistic gymnastics are performed using acrobatics.

Squat To crouch down with your knees bent.

Stamina Staying power – to be able to keep doing exercises without becoming too tired.

Supple The same as flexible.

Tuck To bring your knees up to your chest in a bent position.

Vault To jump over an object.

Warm up To loosen your muscles by stretching before starting on more difficult exercises.

Books to Read

Bellew, Bob. *Gymnastics.* New York: Franklin Watts, 1992.

Haycock, Kate. *Gymnastics.* New York: Macmillan, 1991.

Kuklin, Susan. *Going to My Gymnastics Class.* New York: Macmillan, 1991.

Sullivan, George. *Mary Lou Retton.* New York: Simon & Schuster, 1985.

United States Gymnastics Federation. *Make the Team: Gymnastics for Girls.* New York: Little Brown & Co., 1991.

Washington, Rosemary G. *Gymnastics Is for Me.* Minneapolis: Lerner, 1979.

For further reading, contact the local public library or the organizations listed below. U.S.G.F. publishes a magazine called *U.S.A. Gymnastics.*

Another magazine is *International Gymnast*
225 Brooks
P.O. Box 2450
Oceanside, CA 92051

Useful Addresses

United States Gymnastics Federation
201 South Capital Avenue; Suite 300
Indianapolis, IN 46225

American Turners
1127 East Kentucky Street
P. O. Box 4216
Louisville, KY 40204

President's Council on Physical Fitness
701 Pennsylvania Ave. NW, Suite 250
Washington, DC 20004

American Association on Health, Physical Education, and Dance
1900 Association Drive
Reston, VA 22091

Amateur Athletic Union
3400 West 86 Street
Indianapolis, IN 46268

Or contact your local YMCA, YWCA, gymnastics clubs or schools, or dance schools.

Index